Midday Meals
Around the World

by **Michele Zurakowski**

illustrated by **Jeff Yesh**

Thanks to our advisers for their expertise, research, and advice:

JoAnne Buggey, Ph.D., Elementary Social Studies
College of Education and Human Development
University of Minnesota, Minneapolis
Member, National Council for the Social Studies

Susan Kesselring, M.A., Literacy Educator
Rosemount-Apple Valley-Eagan (Minnesota) School District

PICTURE WINDOW BOOKS
Minneapolis, Minnesota

The editor wishes to thank Susanne Mattison, Culinary Specialist for Byerly's, for her expert advice on preparing the recipes for this book.

Managing Editor: Bob Temple
Creative Director: Terri Foley
Editor: Sara E. Hoffmann
Editorial Adviser: Andrea Cascardi
Copy Editor: Laurie Kahn
Designer: Nathan Gassman
Page production: Picture Window Books
The illustrations in this book were rendered digitally.

Picture Window Books
5115 Excelsior Boulevard
Suite 232
Minneapolis, MN 55416
1-877-845-8392
www.picturewindowbooks.com

To my mother, Ruth Adams Zurakowski,
who taught me to love vegetables
—M.Z.

Printed in the United States of America.

Library of Congress Cataloging-in-Publication Data
Zurakowski, Michele.
Midday meals around the world / by Michele Zurakowski ;
illustrated by Jeff Yesh.
p. cm. — (Meals around the world)
Summary: Discusses the variety of foods people around the world might have for their midday meal.
ISBN 1-4048-0281-9 (hardcover)
ISBN 1-4048-1131-1 (softcover)
1. Luncheons—Juvenile literature.
2. Cookery, International—Juvenile literature.
2. [1. Luncheons. 2. Food habits.] I.Yesh, Jeff, 1971- ill. II. Title.
III. Series.
TX735.Z85 2004
641.5'3—dc22   2003016448

It's almost noon. You haven't eaten since morning. Now your tummy is rumbling, and you feel a little grumpy. It's time for your midday meal!

All around the world, kids get strength and energy from their midday meals.

NORTH AMERICA

UNITED STATES
pages 6-7

MEXICO
page 13

PERU
page 12

SOUTH AMERICA

What are they eating?
Let's travel around
the world and find out!

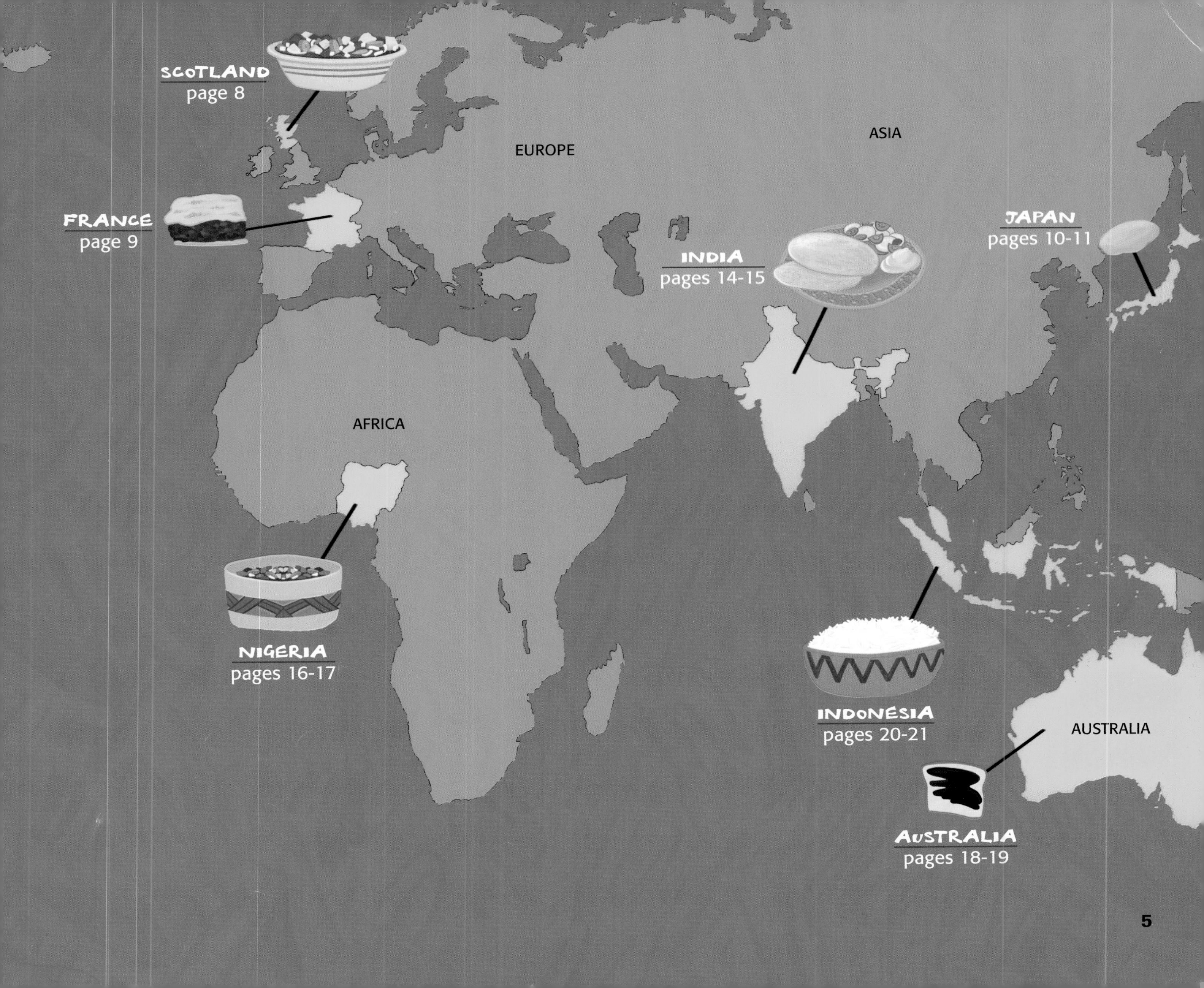

SCOTLAND
page 8

FRANCE
page 9

EUROPE

ASIA

JAPAN
pages 10-11

INDIA
pages 14-15

AFRICA

NIGERIA
pages 16-17

INDONÉSIA
pages 20-21

AUSTRALIA

AUSTRALIA
pages 18-19

5

Peanut butter and jelly sandwiches are pretty popular in the United States. You might like yours fixed in a special way. Some people think jelly is too squishy, so they just have peanut butter on their sandwiches. You might use a cookie cutter to make your sandwich a special shape!

American Midday Meal

- peanut butter
  and jelly sandwich
- apple
- carrot sticks
- milk

Sometimes leftovers make the best meals. In Scotland, lots of families use leftovers to make *stovies*. *Stovies* are a mix of meat and potatoes, and sometimes carrots and onions, too. There's a ton of good stuff in there!

Scottish Midday Meal

• *stovies*
• apple
• milk

How do you feel about hamburger and mashed potatoes? Probably pretty good. What if they were mixed together? In France, kids like to eat *hâchis Parmentier* (ah-SHEE par-mon-tee-AY). That's a fancy name for a dish made of hamburger and mashed potatoes. (If you want to try it, there's a recipe on page 23.)

French Midday Meal

- *hâchis Parmentier*
- *salade de carotte* (carrot salad)
- fruit or yogurt
- water

What if you don't like potatoes or sandwiches? In Japan, kids might have a special kind of rice cake called *onigiri* (oh-NEE-gi-ree) for their midday meals. It's made out of white rice, but that's not all. Inside, there is a yummy surprise—spicy sausage or another kind of meat!

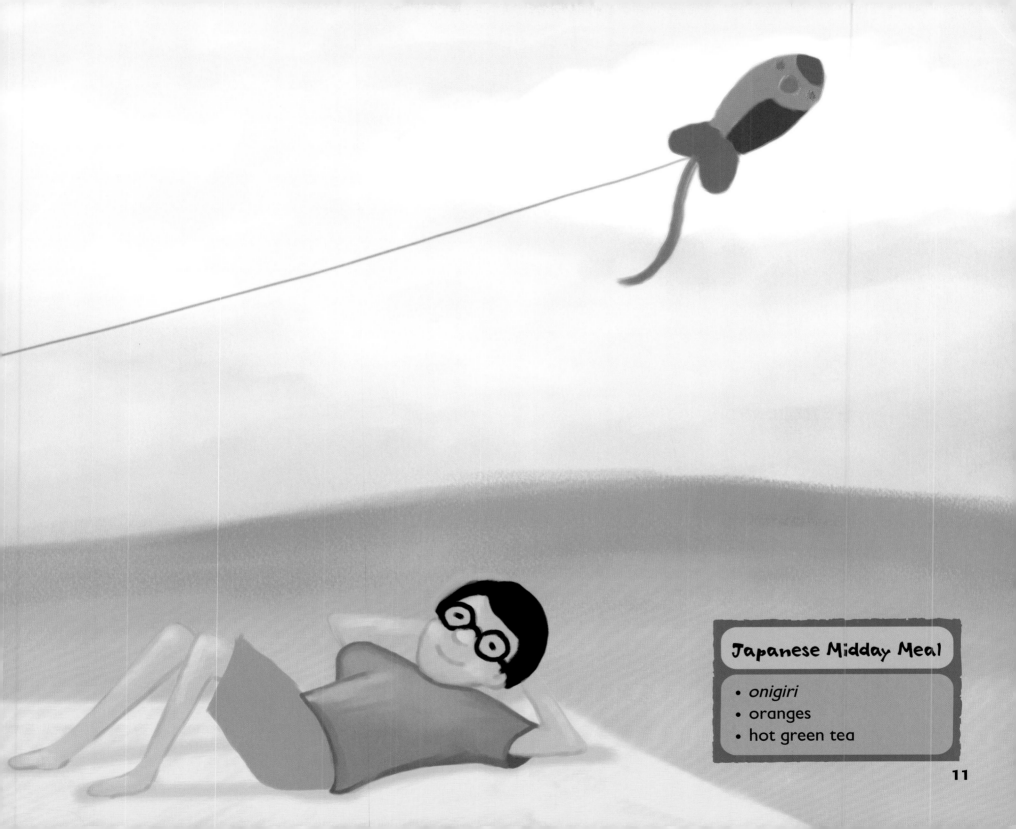

Japanese Midday Meal

- *onigiri*
- oranges
- hot green tea

11

Children in Peru don't often eat snacks, so by the middle of the day, they are hungry. That's OK, because families in Peru like to eat big meals at midday. They might fix juicy steaks.

Peruvian Midday Meal

- steak
- rice
- salad
- fruit

Children in Mexico sometimes get to eat dessert first. Dessert might be a fruit salad. The main course might be a tasty soup with tomatoes and noodles. Sometimes the noodles are even made in the shape of letters!

Mexican Midday Meal

- fruit salad
- tomato and noodle soup
- rice with tomatoes
- corn tortillas
- black beans
- watermelon juice

In India, your parents might not mind if you ate with your hands. In fact, if you're having chapatis (cha-PAH-tees) and vegetables, you're supposed to!

Chapatis are round and flat, like tortillas. You can use them to scoop up your peas and potatoes. Fun!

Indian Midday Meal

- chapatis
- peas and potatoes
- yogurt
- cucumber and tomato salad
- buttermilk

15

In Nigeria, your midday meal would look just as good as it tastes. Children in Nigeria eat big midday meals with their families. They like to have soup and *garri* (gah-REE), a smooth, white porridge.

The soup is full of meat and vegetables. The vegetables in the soup are very colorful—orange, red, green, and yellow. The soup might even be flavored with *ugu* (oo-goo). *Ugu* is a green, leafy vegetable that's kind of like spinach.

Nigerian Midday Meal

- soup
- *garri*
- *popo* (papaya)
- orange
- mango
- tangerine
- water

Instead of peanut butter, children in Australia like to spread Vegemite on their sandwiches.

Vegemite is salty, and it has a strong smell. It's much darker than peanut butter, too. In fact, it's almost black!

Australian Midday Meal

- Vegemite sandwich
- chocolate-covered cookies
- chocolate malted milk

19

Indonesia is a country made up of lots of different islands. Each island has its own special foods, but there's one thing children all across the country like—fried rice.

Indonesians add meat and vegetables to the rice. If they really want to add a special flavor, they might mix in spicy chilies or tart lemongrass.

Indonesian Midday Meal

• fried rice
• fish
• melon
• soup
• coconut milk

21

All around the world, children just like you are getting ready to eat their midday meals. Maybe they will eat big, spicy meals. Maybe they will have bowls of warm porridge.

They might eat with their families. They might eat with their friends at school. Wherever they eat, they are getting energy to keep going. Where would you like to eat *your* midday meal today?

Try These Fun Recipes

You Can Make a Fruit Salad

Makes 4 servings

What you need:

1/2 cup (120 grams) of each of your favorite kinds of fruit—cantaloupe, honeydew, strawberries, and grapes work well

What to do:

1. Cut the different types of fruit into small shapes. For the cantaloupe and honeydew, you might want to use cube shapes. Strawberries can be cut in half. Grapes won't need to be cut at all.

2. Place all of the fruit in a bowl. Stir gently to combine.

Make sure you have an adult to help you.

You Can Make Hâchis Parmentier

Makes 4-6 servings

What you need:

- 1 small onion (optional)
- 1 pound (454 grams) ground beef
- salt and pepper
- 1 teaspoon (5 milliliters) Worcestershire sauce
- 6 cups (1,440 grams) mashed potatoes

What to do:

1. Preheat the oven to 350 degrees Fahrenheit (177 degrees Celsius).

2. Cut the onion (if using) into small pieces. Set aside about 1/2 cup (120 grams) of onion pieces.

3. Cook the meat in a frying pan over medium heat for five minutes. Use a spoon to break it into small pieces.

4. Add the onion (if using). Add a little salt and pepper. Add the Worcestershire sauce. Cook mixture until the onion is clear and the meat is brown all over (about 5-10 minutes).

5. Let the meat mixture cool down.

6. Spread half of the mashed potatoes in the bottom of a pan. Use an 8x8–inch (20x20–centimeter) pan.

7. Cover the potatoes with the meat mixture.

8. Spread the rest of the potatoes on top.

9. Put the pan into the oven to bake. Bake until the dish is hot all the way through (about 15-20 minutes).

Make sure you have an adult to help you.

Fun Facts

- Green tea is a popular drink in Japan. Many people say green tea is good for your heart. It may help fight colds, too.

- Antoine-Augustin Parmentier is the man who brought potatoes to France. He tasted them for the first time when he was in Prussia. He really liked them! He brought the new food to France in 1774. *Hâchis Parmentier* is named after him.

- At schools in Mexico, children might buy tacos with spicy beef and cheese for their midday meals. They also can buy crunchy tostadas with chicken, lettuce, and tomatoes.

- If you like spicy food, you might enjoy eating curry. Curry is a blend of spices that is used to flavor many different foods. It is also the name for a stew-like dish. Curry is popular in India. It makes your mouth tingle!

Glossary

chapati—a round, flat bread that is usually made with whole wheat flour

energy—the strength or power inside us that makes it possible for us to move

porridge—a creamy, hot cereal

tortilla—a kind of Mexican bread made out of wheat or corn. Tortillas are flat and round.

To Learn More

At the Library

Baer, Edith. *This is the Way We Eat Our Lunch: A Book About Children Around the World.* New York: Scholastic, 1995.

Burckhardt, Ann. *The People of Mexico and Their Food.* Mankato, Minn.: Capstone Press, 1996.

Charlip, Remy. *Peanut Butter Party: Including the History, Uses, and Future of Peanut Butter.* Berkeley, Calif.: Tricycle Press, 1999.

Compestine, Ying Chang. *The Story of Chopsticks.* New York: Holiday House, 2001.

Dooley, Norah. *Everybody Cooks Rice.* Minneapolis: Carolrhoda Books, 1991.

Fact Hound

Fact Hound offers a safe, fun way to find Web sites related to this book. All of the sites on Fact Hound have been researched by our staff.
http://www.facthound.com

1. Visit the Fact Hound home page.
2. Enter a search word related to this book, or type in this special code: 1404802819.
3. Click on the FETCH IT button.

Your trusty Fact Hound will fetch the best sites for you!

Index